# Baby Birthday Parties

## PENNY WARNER

Meadowbrook Press

Distributed by Simon & Schuster
New York

Library of Congress Cataloging-in-Publication Data
Warner, Penny.
    Baby birthday parties / Penny Warner.
        p.     cm.
    ISBN 0-88166-349-2 (Meadowbrook)—ISBN 0-689-83150-1 (Simon & Schuster)
    1. Children's parties. 2. Birthdays. I. Title.
  GV1205.W374     1999
  793.2'1—dc21                              99-37105
                                                      CIP

Editors: Liya Lev Oertel, Christine Zuchora-Walske
Copyeditor: Nancy Campbell
Proofreader: Joseph Gredler
Production Manager: Joe Gagne
Desktop Publishing: Danielle White
Cover Art: Amanda Haley
Illustrations: Laurel Aiello

Published by Meadowbrook Press, 5451 Smetana Drive, Minnetonka, MN 55343

www.meadowbrookpress.com

BOOK TRADE DISTRIBUTION by Simon & Schuster, a division of Simon and Schuster, Inc., 1230 Avenue of the Americas, New York, NY 10020

04 03 02 01 00 99  10 9 8 7 6 5 4 3 2 1

Printed in the United States of America

# CONTENTS

# DEDICATION

To Tom, Matt, and Rebecca

# ACKNOWLEDGMENTS

I want to thank all my students at Diablo Valley College, Chabot College, and Ohlone College for their generous contributions. Thanks to the second and third generation of babies: Jonathan Ellington, Mia Ellington, Steven Ellington, Geoffie Pike, Samuel Valdez, Zachary Valdez, Chloe Webster, Dakota Webster, and Levi Webster. Thanks to Sue Stadelhofer for her enthusiasm. Thanks to Ed Pike for Buddy Boy. And a special thanks to my publisher, Bruce Lansky, and my editor, Liya Lev Oertel, and everyone at Meadowbrook Press for everything they do for me.

# INTRODUCTION

It's your baby's first birthday! And you want to celebrate this very special event with your baby, your family, and your friends. But is your baby too young to have a party? Absolutely not!

While plenty of books on the market help parents plan their older children's birthday parties, this is the first book to provide birthday party ideas for babies ages one to three years!

As a child-development instructor and kids' party planner, I've made a special effort to keep the party themes appropriate to babies' interests and developmental levels. And I've made the party plans easy for parents and fun for babies.

You'll find twenty birthday party ideas for babies, from Animal Adventures to Winter Wonderland. Each party comes complete with suggestions for simple costumes, easy invitations, quick decorations, fun games and activities, yummy snacks, creative cakes, and inexpensive favors to send home with guests. I've also included variations on the party themes, for even more birthday party possibilities. And you'll find helpful hints at the end of each party, to help keep the festivities running smoothly.

It's never too soon to celebrate your baby's most important day! So pick a party that's perfect for your baby, and let the fun begin!

# HELPFUL HINTS FOR A SUCCESSFUL PARTY

## PARTY PLANNING

- Keep the party short and sweet (an hour to an hour and a half) to match your guests' short attention spans. Children ages one to three get cranky if they're kept awake too long.
- In general, the best times for most babies are late morning (after the morning nap) or late afternoon (following the afternoon nap). To plan the party when your child is most alert, pay attention to your child's day to discover the optimum times.
- Try to plan the party for a weekend. The babies won't care what day you select, but a weekend party is usually more convenient for the adults who will attend.
- Be sure to include the parents as guests, so they can help their own children participate in the fun.
- Invite a small number of children to the party—from one to three is ideal, and five is the maximum. Over five young guests may put the party at risk of deteriorating into an almost unmanageable gathering with a fair amount of crying.
- Get extra help—babysitter, grandparent, or friend—so you can participate in the party activities and share the fun with your child.
- Take lots of pictures, but avoid shooting flash photos too often. Camera flashes can irritate babies and make them edgy. Be sure to use film that photographs well in indoor lighting.

## PROVIDE BREAKS DURING THE PARTY

- Some babies have difficulty handling the extra excitement and attention at parties. To help keep your child calm and relaxed, be sure to give him or her a nap or rest period before—and after—the party. In addition, allow for some "time off" during the party—such as a break in the kitchen alone with you while you prepare the treats.

- If other children have trouble handling the excitement, tell the parents they are free to take a break from the party, too, such as a walk around the block or some time in the backyard.
- If your child cries or has a tantrum during the party, take him or her to another room to provide a break from the noise and activity. Then give your child something specific to do for the party to help ease into more cooperative behavior. Doing a simple chore helps relieve tension, distract attention from a problem, and make a child feel more in control.

## KEEP GUESTS OCCUPIED

- Have extra playthings on hand to amuse the young ones and lots of favors that guests can take home. They will delight in having something new and be less likely to be jealous of the honored child's gifts.
- Some babies prefer the gift-wrap to the gift, the frosting to the cake, and the old toys to the new toys. That's perfectly normal—let your child enjoy the party his or her way.
- If guests don't want to participate in the fun and games or food, don't force it. Some babies simply need time to adjust to the novelty and excitement of a party. Many prefer to watch the fun—and they enjoy the party just as much!
- Ask the birthday child to pass around the gifts, and promise him or her that they will come back! If the birthday child doesn't want to share the new toys, set out a box of toys the other children can play with. Or, give the guests their favors early in the party, so they can play with them during the party and then take the favors home.

## FOOD

- Check with parents to make sure their children don't have any food allergies, and do your best to avoid using any of the allergy-causing items in the party food. If that is not possible, let the parents know which foods are off-limits for their child. If you have pets, be sure to discuss animal allergies as well, making any needed adjustments.
- Keep treats simple, but decorate and package them creatively; the snacks should be fun, but safe to eat.

## GO WITH THE FLOW

- If your child dozes off during the party, let him or her sleep. Some babies shut down if there's too much excitement. Keep an eye on the sleeping guest of honor while entertaining the rest of the guests.
- Roll with the unexpected. If the guests like the props of the game better than the game itself, let them make up their own play. If they won't touch the food you've prepared, they won't starve. If they want to go home, they can go home. If they won't leave parents' laps, they can still enjoy the party. And if they fight, it will be over in a few seconds and they'll soon be friends again.

## WRAP IT UP

- When departure time arrives, mention that it's getting close to your child's rest time and begin to clean up and get out the good-bye goodie bags. This should help wrap things up for those parents who want to linger. It's important for you and your child to have some time alone after the event, and for the party not to seem endless.
- After the party is over and your child is asleep, sit down, put your feet up, and enjoy the memories of this very special occasion. You can clean up the mess when your child wakes up—that's half the fun for him or her!

# ANIMAL ADVENTURE PARTY

Host the perfect party for babies with an Animal Adventure theme and let the cute and cuddly stuffed critters join in the fun!

## INVITATIONS

- Animated Animals: Cut out pictures of animals from inexpensive children's books or draw them yourself. Fold a piece of construction paper in half and paste the animal cutouts on the front. Glue on wiggly eyes, feathers, and other three-dimensional details. Draw a speech bubble with a dark felt-tip pen and fill it with a party greeting, such as "Come to an Animal Adventure Party!" Write the rest of the details inside the fold and mail to guests.
- Baby Animals: Buy small plastic animals at a toy store and tie each party invitation to a toy with ribbon. Mail in padded envelopes to the guests. The guest baby can play with the toy while parents read the invitation.

(Make sure that the toys are not too small, so children won't swallow them.)

## DECORATIONS

- Animal Posters: Buy posters of baby animals and hang them on the walls of the party room at a young child's eye level.
- Animal Centerpiece: Assemble a variety of stuffed animals on the

them on the guests' heads when they arrive. Costume shops and toy stores offer a variety of animal headbands—with bear ears, mouse ears, rabbit ears, and so on. If you prefer, make your own animal headbands: Make animal ears from stiff construction paper and glue them onto plain, store-bought headbands.

## GAMES

- Tape the Trunk: For babies, bigger is better, so enlarge "Pin the Tail on the Donkey" into "Tape the Trunk on the Elephant." Buy two identical elephant posters and cut out the trunk of one. That will be the trunk your guests will tape onto the intact elephant poster with double-sided tape. (If you are artistically inclined, draw your own elephant on a large sheet of poster board and make the trunk out of construction paper.) Explain the game to the players. Have the first player wear a large hat to cover her eyes (instead of a blindfold), give her the trunk with

table to form a centerpiece. If you like, buy or make a paper tablecloth that looks like a forest or farm and set the animals on top. Or cover the table with a piece of fabric decorated with animals.

## COSTUMES

- Make or buy headbands with attached animal ears and place

a piece of double-sided tape on the back, and stand her a foot or so from the elephant poster. Then help her find her way. If she peeks, it's okay!

- What's That Noise? Buy a recording of animal sounds. Have the little ones sit in a circle. Play the sounds and have them guess what animal makes each sound.
- Act Like an Animal: Have the guests sit in a circle, then have the parents act out an animal's movements. Ask the kids to guess the animal.

## KING OF THE JUNGLE CAKE

1. Use a cake mold to create a lion cake.
2. Frost with yellow icing.
3. Add eyes, mouth, teeth, nose, whiskers, and other details with candies or icing.
4. Set small plastic animals around the bottom of the cake. (Or make a sheet cake, frost with green icing, and decorate the top with plastic animals.)

## ACTIVITIES

- Make-a-Mask: Cut out face shapes from fun foam or heavy construction paper. Cut out holes for eyes, noses, and mouths. Use your own child's face to estimate the distances between the eyes, nose, and mouth. Then glue or staple a tongue depressor stick at the bottom of each face to serve as a handle. Provide nontoxic felt-tip pens for coloring the masks, as well as a variety of decorative items like sequins, feathers, and glitter for gluing onto the mask. Then let the guests make their own masks. When they finish, have an animal parade.

- Home Zoo: Hire an animal trainer to come to the party with a real animal, such as a pony, a goat, or an exotic bird for the kids to learn about, play with, and pet.
- Animal Faces: Hire a face painter (or nominate yourself) to paint the kids' faces to look like lions, tigers, and bears—oh my! Use nontoxic face paints, then add ears and ribbon tails to complete the look.

## FOOD

- Serve zoo food to the babies at a help-yourself buffet for animals. Include a bowl of Animal Crackers, Monkey Bites (banana pieces), Chimp Chips (potato chips), Python Pieces (fruit strips), Rabbit Pellets (raisins), Cheetah Cheese (cheese cubes), and Pet Peas (frozen green peas, cooked briefly and cooled).
- Serve chocolate milk in small bowls for some more animal fun.

- Set out a "Do Not Feed the Animals" sign, but cross off the "Not."

## FAVORS

- Send your guests home with small stuffed animals, Beanie Babies, small plastic animals, or animal books.
- Hand out safari hats filled with animal toys and animal crackers.

## VARIATIONS

- Take the kids to a petting zoo and let them see real animals. Ask parents to help with supervision.
- Watch a video about animals, such as *The Lion King* or *Babe*.

## HELPFUL HINTS

- Make sure that all toys are big enough so they won't be swallowed, and that all animal features are securely fastened to the toys.
- Ask guests' parents to help at the party.
- Keep in mind that some babies are afraid of masks, so adjust the activity if needed.

# BABES IN TOYLAND PARTY

What better place to have a party for babies than in Toyland? All your guests will need to enjoy themselves is a bunch of fun toys!

## INVITATIONS

- Cootie Catcher: Take a square of construction paper and fold it in half. Open it and fold it in half in the opposite direction. Open again and fold all four corners to meet in the center. Turn the paper over and fold all four corners to meet in the center. Fold the paper in half, with the meeting corners on the inside. Open and fold in half again in the opposite direction. Gently insert thumbs and index fingers under the flaps that are a single thickness of paper. Press fingers together to lift the flaps and make the Cootie Catcher work. Now open the paper and write the party details on the different sections of the Cootie Catcher. Fold back up and mail to guests.

- Use colorful ribbons to attach party invitations to small toys. Mail in padded envelopes.

## DECORATIONS

- Toyland: Cut out pictures of toys from catalogs or inexpensive picture books and tape them to the lower half of the walls, at a baby's eye level.
- Set out stuffed animals and toys on the floor.

- Make a toy centerpiece on the table.
- Decorate the ceiling with colorful crepe-paper streamers to add to the Toyland atmosphere.

## COSTUMES

- When guests arrive, give them headbands with wiggly antennae or little caps with pinwheels on top.

## GAMES

- Puzzle Put-Together: Provide a collection of wooden puzzles and let the kids put them together. You can buy puzzles, have parents bring puzzles from home, or borrow them from a toy-lending library. You can even make your own puzzles from heavy construction paper and colorful pictures.
- Ball Game: Collect a variety of balls, such as beach balls, tennis balls, Ping-Pong balls, yarn balls, rubber balls, soccer balls, pompoms, and Nerf balls. Have the children sit in a large circle, give each one a ball, and let them throw, push, or toss the balls to one another.
- Toy Hide-and-Seek: Buy a bunch of small, inexpensive toys and hide them all over the party room. Let the babies try to find them. When a child finds a toy, he gets to keep it; then he drops out of the game so everyone gets to find a toy.
- Toy Chase: Tie a string to a toy and set the toy in the middle of the room. Pull the string and

have the children try to catch the toy. When a child catches a toy, he gets to keep it; then he drops out of the game so the others can each catch a toy.

## ACTIVITIES

- Make-a-Toy: Collect paper-towel tubes before the party. Buy small balls that fit inside the

### ABC BLOCK CAKE

1. Bake a sheet cake, cool, and cut into six squares.
2. Stack the squares in pairs to make three cubes of cake. Cover each cube with a different color of frosting.
3. Using contrasting-colored icing, write a letter A on the top and sides of one cake cube, write the letter B on the next cake, and write the letter C on the last cake.
4. Set B and C cakes next to each other, with B on the left and C on the right. Then set the A cake on top of the B and C cakes. Place small toy blocks around the bottom of the cake.

tubes. When the young guests arrive, give them paints, felt-tip pens, glitter, construction paper, or stickers to decorate the tubes. When the tubes are finished, show the kids how to place a ball at the top of a tube and let it fall out the other end. If two people play together, one can drop the ball and the other can try to catch it.

- Toyland: Set a large sheet of cardboard or particleboard on the floor. Paint streets and lakes on the board. Then set out all kinds of toys, blocks, balls, cars, stuffed animals, tiny people, and so on. Let kids work together to create their own Toyland using the board as a background.

## FOOD

- Assemble a Mr. Potato Head as a centerpiece, and serve a bowl of chips next to him. Let the kids make their own potato heads with real potatoes. Provide a cooled baked potato for each guest, cut the potatoes open, and let kids make faces using cut-up veggies and bacon bits, with shredded cheese for hair.
- Make peanut-butter-and-jelly sandwiches, then remove crusts and cut them into quarters to make Block Bites. Stack the Block Bites to make a building or a tower.
- Serve Clown Salad: Place canned pear halves cut side down on plates covered with lettuce. Make clown faces using grated cheese for hair, raisins for eyes, cherries for noses, and raisins for mouths.

## FAVORS

- Send the guests home with small toys, such as balls, blocks, figures, puzzles, animals, Slinkies, stuffed animals, and so on.

- Hand out homemade picture frames with photos of each guest. Before the party, make picture frames from poster board (sizing the opening slightly smaller than a photo produced by a Polaroid camera), cover the frames with colored paper, and glue on magnetic alphabet letters to spell each guest's name. Take Polaroid snapshots of the kids during the party and place the photos into the frames.

## VARIATIONS

- Show videos with toy themes, such as *Babes in Toyland, Toy Story,* or *The Toy.*
- Go to a toy exhibit, such as a Lego show. (Make sure to have plenty of adult supervision.)

## HELPFUL HINTS

- Provide enough toys for all the kids to play with during the party, so no one has to share.
- Have at least one toy for each guest to take home.
- Make sure toys are age-appropriate and unbreakable.

# BARNEY'S DINOSAUR PARTY

Join Barney and his friends at a Dinosaur Party, and bring those extinct creatures back to life for some fun and games!

## INVITATIONS

- Egg Surprise: Write party details on a small, white, egg-shaped piece of paper. Insert the paper and a small plastic dinosaur into a small plastic egg that opens and closes. Glue a Barney picture on the outside of the egg, being careful not to put glue on the opening edges of the egg. Mail to guests in padded envelopes.
- Cracked Egg: Fold a large sheet of heavy white construction paper in half. Draw a large egg shape on one half, with the top of the egg on the fold. Cut out the egg through both halves, leaving the fold intact, to make an egg-shaped card. Photocopy a picture of the birthday child and glue the photocopy inside the card. Write party details around

the picture. Mail to guests, who will "crack" the egg open for a surprise invitation inside.

## DECORATIONS

- Create a Land of the Barneys:
  –Cut out large footprints from construction paper and place them on the front walk, leading to the party house.

–Line the walls with sheets of purple crepe paper.

## COSTUMES

- Turn guests into dinosaurs. Paint their faces green and spotty, attach a jagged tail, and top them off with a cracked-egg hat made from old knitted caps or empty gallon milk jugs cut with a scalloped edge.

## GAMES

- Barney-Tail Limbo: Cut out a large purple tail (shaped like Barney's tail) from poster board. Play Barney music while you hold the tail horizontally in the air. Have the kids walk or crawl under the Barney Tail, then lower it each time they pass by.
- Barney's Missing! Collect three to five Barney products, such as a doll, a book, a picture, an action figure, and so on, as long as each one has a picture of Barney on it. Set the items in the center of the room with the babies seated around them. Point out and describe each item to the babies, then cover the items with a blanket. Pick

–Hang posters of Barney on the walls at a baby's eye level.

–Play Barney songs in the background.

–Set out toy Barneys as a table centerpiece.

–Buy Barney paper products at a party store.

–Swag purple crepe-paper streamers from the ceiling.

up one item together with the blanket, keeping the item covered, and reveal the remaining items. Ask the children which Barney item is missing.

- Color-Me Barney Puzzle: Trace an outline of Barney on white construction paper. Cut the Barney out and then cut him into puzzle parts, such as arms, legs, head, and so on—one puzzle piece for each child. Distribute the pieces and have

## BARNEY EGG CAKE

1. Bake a round cake; allow to cool.
2. Cut the cake with a knife down the middle in a zigzag pattern, to look like a cracked egg. Pull the egg apart a little.
3. Cover the cake with white frosting.
4. Insert a small Barney in the cracked opening, as though he is just coming out of the cracked egg. Set little Barneys all around the bottom of the cake.

the guests color their pieces with purple crayons. When everyone is finished, try to put Barney together!

- Dino Dig: Hide dinosaurs in a sandbox, either inside plastic eggs or by themselves. Let the young ones dig for dinosaurs and keep what they find. If no sandbox is available, use a large shallow box or box lid filled with packing peanuts. Watch kids closely to be sure no sand or packing peanuts get near their mouths!

- Follow the Footsteps: Cut out large dinosaur footprints and set them a few inches apart all around the house. Place one Barney item every few feet for the babies to discover. Have them follow the footprints to the hidden prizes.

## ACTIVITIES

- Surprise Dinosaur Eggs: Buy some medium-sized white plastic eggs. Fill the eggs with gummy dinosaurs, dinosaur fruit snacks, or dinosaur cookies. Close the eggs and give them to the babies to decorate with stickers. Then have them open the eggs for a surprise inside!
- Barney—Live! Hire a performer dressed as Barney to make a surprise appearance. Or rent the costume at a costume shop and dress up yourself.

## FOOD

- Make Colorful Dino Eggs: Hard-boil eggs and let them cool. Prepare egg dyes and help the children dye the eggs. Then give them stickers to decorate their eggs. When they finish, have

them crack the eggs open and eat them. (Supervise this, to make sure the kids don't eat any shell.) If your guests don't want to break their eggs, have some backup eggs ready to eat.
- Serve Barney Sandwiches: Cut out dinosaur-shaped cheese and bread slices with dinosaur cookie cutters. Assemble the slices into sandwiches and serve to hungry dinosaur eaters.

## FAVORS

- Send the dinosaur kids home with anything Barney: dolls, books, pictures, posters, stickers, hats, and so on.
- Let guests keep the Barney toys they find during the games.

## VARIATIONS

- Watch a Barney video or have a Barney sing-along.

## HELPFUL HINTS

- Be sure to have enough Barney toys for everyone.
- Avoid small toys or toys with detachable parts, to prevent the kids choking on the toys.

# BEACH BABIES PARTY

Have a backyard beach party for your baby, with lots of sun, sand, and water fun!

## INVITATIONS

- Buoys and Gulls: Photocopy your baby's picture and cut it into a circle. Fold a white sheet of paper into a card, and glue the photo onto the front. Glue a circle of rope around the picture so baby is inside a life buoy. Draw or glue on pictures of gulls. On the front of the card, write "You're invited to a Beach Babies Party, Buoys and Gulls!" Inside write the party details.
- Picture Postcards: Buy postcards featuring pictures of beaches. Write details of the party on the left side of the card and the guest's name on the right. Mail to guests.

## DECORATIONS

- Set up the sandbox and deco-rate it with leis and crepe-paper streamers.
- Set out the kiddie pool and fill it with tepid water.

- Cut out giant colorful fish made from construction paper or posters, and hang them on a fence or hedge at a baby's eye level.
- Add scallops of blue crepe-paper streamers along the top of the fence or hedge to simulate ocean waves.
- Spread a beach towel over the picnic table for a tablecloth, and place seashells down its center.
- Set out pails and shovels, beach balls, and other beach toys.

toss and catch the balloons. As the balloons go splat, the babies get wet! Then let the kids throw the water balloons at the parents and try to get them wet!

- Bird Squirter: Buy an inexpensive squirt bottle for each guest. Make eyes at the top of the squirt bottle, using the nozzle as the beak. Let the children cover the bottle with stickers and fill the bottles with water. Let them go outside and squirt their birds.
- Water Snake: Turn on the hose and move the stream of water back and forth over a small area. Have the kids try to run across the wiggly line without getting their feet wet!
- Water Jump: Turn on the hose and hold the water stream an inch from the ground. Have the kids take turns jumping over the water. Raise the water an inch each time they complete a jump. Have one or two parents close by to catch anyone who starts to fall.

## COSTUMES

- Ask each guest to wear a bathing suit and to bring a beach wrap and a change of clothing.

## GAMES

- Don't Get Wet! Set up sprinklers and have the kids try to run through without getting wet. Turn the sprinklers on and off as they attempt to get to the other side.
- Water Balloon Toss: Fill small balloons with water. Line up your guests and have them try to

## ACTIVITIES

- Build a Sandcastle: Put the babies in a sandbox and have them build a sandcastle. Provide them with small buckets of water to moisten and mold the sand, and teach them how to make a castle.
- Beach Ball Chase: Buy enough beach balls to have one for each guest. (They make great favors to send home!) Have kids stand in a large circle facing away from the middle. Set all the balls in the middle. On the count of three, have them turn around and run to the middle to try to grab a ball.

## BEACH CAKE

1. Bake a sheet cake and allow to cool.
2. Frost half the cake with blue frosting to make an ocean.
3. Frost the other half with chocolate frosting, then sprinkle with brown sugar to look like sand.
4. Build a sandcastle with brown sugar cubes.
5. Add plastic sharks coming out of the water.

- Beach Ball Catch: Have kids stand in a circle. Give one player a beach ball and have him toss it to a player next to him. That player has to catch the ball and toss it to the next player. Go around the circle once, then add a second ball for more fun!
- Buried Treasure: Bury toys in a sandbox and have the kids try to find them.
- Sand Play: Give the guests pails, shovels, sifters, shakers, pourers, cups, spoons, and other items to enjoy in the sand, and just let them play.
- Go Fish: Make fishing poles using short sticks with string tied to one end. Tie a magnet to the other end of the string. Place toys with attached

magnets into the kiddie pool, and let each child fish for a toy.

## FOOD

- Serve Ants in the Sand: Crush graham crackers to a sandy consistency. Pour into a baggie until one-third to one-half full. Add a dash of chocolate sprinkles to each baggie. Give the kids their baggies and let them eat the "sand" with their fingers. (Be sure they eat this treat outside!)
- Let your guests eat from a fish bowl! Find a fish bowl or a clear bowl. Make blue or green Jell-O and pour into bowl. Add gummy fish to the Jell-O and place the bowl in the refrigerator to set. Or make individual fish bowls for each guest.
- Make your own rainbow Popsicles: Mix red Kool-Aid and pour into small paper cups, filling one-third full. Cover the cups with foil, then poke a Popsicle stick into the center of each cup so the stick stands straight up. Let set in freezer until firm. Then mix lemon Kool-Aid and pour over the red layers, filling the cups two-thirds full. Let set. Mix blue or green Kool-Aid, pour on top of the lemon layers until the cups are full, then let set. When the top layers are firm, peel off the paper cups and serve to kids.
- Serve fish sticks with a side of Goldfish crackers for lunch.

## FAVORS

- Send the beach babies home with water toys, sand toys, plastic sunglasses, small towels, seashells, or beach balls.

## VARIATIONS

- Go to the beach. Be sure to bring along guests' parents to watch the kids.
- Watch *The Little Mermaid* on video.

## HELPFUL HINTS

- Put sun block on the babies and reapply it often.
- Watch out for slippery ground.
- WATCH KIDS CAREFULLY around water and sand. Be sure to have extra help at the party for safety.

# BIG TOP PARTY

Bring the babies under the Big Top for some clowning around at the circus!

## INVITATIONS

- Clown Face: Write party details on the back of a white paper plate. Photocopy a clown face and glue it to the other side of the plate, or draw one using a picture of a clown as a model. Use a felt-tip pen to add a funny mouth, wide-open eyes, and other facial details like freckles or rosy cheeks. Glue yarn hair at the top and a bow tie at the bottom. Then glue a red pompom in the middle of the face to make a nose. Mail in a padded envelope.

## DECORATIONS

- Set up a circus tent: Swag colorful crepe-paper streamers from the center of the ceiling to the corners and sides of the room, and let them dangle down the walls.
- Place animal posters on the walls at a baby's eye level.
- Place three Hula-Hoops on the floor to make a three-ring performance area.
- Cut two large appliance boxes into cages and paint them with bright colors or cover them with animal-print paper or cloth. Set the cages in the party room with stuffed animals inside.
- Decorate the table with toy clowns, small plastic circus animals, and a carousel cake.
- Play marching music in the background.

## COSTUMES

- Make, rent, or buy clown accessories, such as big feet, red

Give the children beanbags or balls to try to throw through the holes on the clown face.

- Knock Down the Animals: Set up a row of stuffed animals on the floor or table. Have your guests take turns rolling a ball at the stuffed animals. If a player knocks over an animal, she gets to keep the stuffed animal. Then another player takes a turn. Let the guests roll until everyone gets an animal.
- Copy the Clown: Have an adult dress up like a clown. Then have the clown lead the group in a game of Simon Says or Copy Cat.

## ACTIVITIES

- Clown Face: Have a face painter come to the party and turn all the baby faces into clown faces.
- Animal Masks: Buy sheets of craft foam in animal colors (black, tan, brown, gray, and so on). Cut the foam into circles the size of a baby's face, and cut out eye and mouth holes. Staple or Super Glue a ribbon at each side, for tying the mask in the back. Search for large animal

noses, bow ties, orange or yellow wigs, and white gloves. Offer them to your guests as they arrive. (Party stores and costume shops are good sources for such items.)

## GAMES

- Toss the Clown Nose: Get a large cardboard box and paint the front of the box to look like a clown face. Cut out the eyes, the nose, and the mouth, making wide holes; set the box in the middle of the party room.

faces on posters and calendars, or in books and magazines. Copy, if necessary, and then cut out the animal eyes, noses, mouths, and ears. Let the kids

## CLOWN CUPCAKES

1. Bake cupcakes and allow to cool.
2. Remove paper baking cups from the cupcakes.
3. Take clean paper baking cups, flatten them, and set cupcakes in the middle.
4. Frost cupcakes with white icing; the frosted cakes will be the clown face, and the flattened cups are clown collars.
5. Decorate the clown heads and faces with tubes of colored icing.

## CLOWN CONES

1. Fill sugar cones with balls of ice cream and place upside down on flattened paper baking cups. The cones are the hats and the balls of ice cream are the faces.
2. Add face details with icing.
3. Serve with Clown Cupcakes.

glue the cutouts near the openings on the foam circles to make animal faces. Have your guests wear their masks and play at being animals—and don't forget to take pictures.

- Circus Juggler: Hire a juggler to come to the party and perform amazing juggling feats. Or hire a clown magician for the party.
- Balloon Animals: Hire someone to make balloon animals for all the kids.
- Circus Stunts: Have the kids perform simple stunts, such as a somersault, a tightrope walk on a balance beam (or on a piece of tape on the floor for one- and two-year-olds), a headstand against

the wall, an animal walk, or a step through a Hula-Hoop. Videotape the stunts and play back the video for the party guests.

## FOOD

- Make Elephant and Monkey (peanut butter and banana) sandwiches for your hungry clowns. Serve with a side of Chocolate Tiger's Milk.
- Serve Monkey on a Stick: Stick bananas on Popsicle sticks, freeze, then serve. If you like, roll the frozen bananas in peanut butter and sprinkle with crisped rice cereal.
- Make or buy giant pretzels and serve with melted cheese or mild mustard. Or make the pretzels with the kids as a party activity: Prepare the dough and have your guests shape pieces of the dough into any shapes they like; then bake, cool, and serve.

## FAVORS

- Send your guests home with small toy clowns and plastic circus animals.
- Insert small toys inside deflated large balloons. Inflate the balloons and give them to the kids as they leave.
- Give your small clowns clown accessories, such as clown noses, bow ties, hats, feet, and gloves.
- Fill bags with small toys, candies, and books about the circus. Tie the bags with ribbons and attach big red clown noses labeled with the guests' names.

## VARIATIONS

- Take the kids to a local circus, carnival, or fair. Be sure to have lots of adult supervision.

## HELPFUL HINTS

- Crepe paper goes a long way in creating a circus atmosphere.
- Some babies are afraid of clowns, so introduce the clown slowly. If necessary, ask the clown to remove the wig, nose, and other accessories to show your guests that this strange creature is actually a person.

# BUBBLES AND BALLOONS PARTY

For babies, bubbles and balloons are magical. So host a party with lots of pop!

## INVITATIONS

- Blow-Up Balloons: Draw a funny face on one side of an inflated balloon. Write party details on the other side with a permanent felt-tip pen. Deflate the balloon, insert in an envelope, and mail. Each guest must inflate the balloon to read the invitation and see the funny face!
- Balloon Bouquet: Cut out small circles from different colors of construction paper or sheets of craft foam. Glue the circles together, slightly overlapping, to form a Balloon Bouquet. Glue strands of colored ribbon to the bottom of each balloon. Write party details on the back and mail in a large envelope.
- Buy small packets of bubble bath. Write party details on a small sheet of paper and glue to

the back of the bubble-bath packet. Mail.

## DECORATIONS

- Fill the ceiling with helium balloons.
- Inflate balloons, rub them on your shirt or hair, then stick them to the walls (or use double-sided tape).

table, with each baby's name written on top.
- Make a balloon bouquet of real balloons for the centerpiece.

## COSTUMES
- Tie a helium balloon to the back of each baby so the balloon always follows him. (Keep the string short so he doesn't get tangled.)
- Draw balloons or bubbles on the babies' faces with face paints.
- Hand out T-shirts painted with balloons and bubbles.

## GAMES
- Pop the Bubble: Have several parents blow bubbles for the guests to pop. Make giant bubbles using larger blowers and let the babies and toddlers take turns trying to pop the big bubbles.
- Catch the Balloon: Inflate balloons, toss them in the air, and have the guests try to catch them as they fall.
- Guess the Balloon Animal: Hire a balloon animal magician to make balloon animals. Let the babies guess the animal after it is finished.

- Cut out giant balloons from colored construction paper and place on the walls at a baby's eye level.
- Have someone blow bubbles to greet the guests as they arrive.
- Rent a bubble maker and set it on the table to keep the bubbles coming.
- Cut out colored balloons for place mats and set them on the

- Sticky Balloons: Using double-faced tape, stick a balloon on the back of each baby. Let the babies try to grab each other's balloons.
- Chase the Balloon: Tie a long string to a balloon and set the balloon in the middle of the floor. Take the string and go to another room. Pull the balloon slowly and have the babies chase the balloon.

## ACTIVITIES

- Big Bubbles: Buy bubble solution (or make your own with dish soap) and pour into a large bucket. Hand out giant bubble blowers and let the kids make their own Big Bubbles.
- Face Balloons: Give each child a felt-tip pen and a balloon, and let everyone draw funny faces on their balloons. Draw and cut out feet from construction paper and tape them to the bottoms of the balloons so the funny faces will stand when they're finished.
- Bubble Painting: Place a small amount of poster paint in a small cup. Add a straw. Teach the kids how to blow (not suck) through the straw. Then have them blow into the cup of paint to make millions of bubbles. After the bubbles come bubbling

## BALLOON CAKE

1. Follow a favorite recipe to make a round cake. (If you like, bake the cake in an ovenproof bowl, then turn it onto a plate, curved-side up, to look like a balloon.)
2. Frost with favorite icing.
3. Decorate with plastic balloons on top and around the sides.

over the top, capture them by placing a white sheet of paper over the cup. The bubbles will pop onto the paper, leaving colorful circles. Rotate paint colors (and blowers) to make a multicolored design.

## FOOD

- Make Balloon Cookies with Licorice Strings: Make sugar-cookie dough and divide it into thirds. Tint one-third red, one-third blue, and one-third yellow. Roll out the dough and cut balloon shapes using a drinking glass. Bake and cool. When done, attach a string of licorice to the back of each cookie using a small bit of icing as glue.
- Serve bubbly drinks and stick crazy straws into the drinks for fun.
- Offer Balloon Sandwiches: Have a bakery tint two loaves of bread, one pink and one blue. Cut bread slices into large circles. For your sandwiches, take one slice of each color and fill with peanut butter and jelly, cheese and bologna, or tuna.

## FAVORS

- Send the kids home with their very own Mylar balloons.
- Give them bubble solution to take home.
- Let them keep their Balloon Animals.

## VARIATION

- Hire a Balloon Clown or Magician to entertain the kids.

## HELPFUL HINTS

- If you plan to concentrate on blowing bubbles, you might want to host this party outdoors. If so, be sure any helium balloons are secured tightly so they cannot sail away and pollute the environment.
- Be sure to watch babies around balloons, so they don't put popped or deflated balloons in their mouths and choke. If a balloon pops, pick up and throw away all the pieces immediately.
- Ask parents to help sooth any babies who might be startled by the sudden loud pop of a balloon.

# BUSY BUILDERS PARTY

Keep those busy hands creatively occupied at a Busy Builders Party. All you need are some construction toys to build a whole new world!

## INVITATIONS

- Building Blocks: Cut out six large block shapes from different-colored construction paper. On the front of each block write one of the following words: "Come" "to" "a" "Busy" "Builders" "Party!" On the back of the blocks write the party details. Mail all six blocks together for the parent and guest to build the invitation before reading.
- Lego My Invitation: Cut out pictures of Legos from toy catalogs. Glue them to the front of a folded piece of paper. Write the party details inside. Attach a Lego or Duplo block and mail.

## DECORATIONS

- Cut out big blocks from colored construction paper. Write guests' names on each block. Tape to the walls at a baby's eye level.

- Set out building materials, such as Legos, blocks, wood scraps (rough edges sanded), Tinker Toys, Bristle Blocks, and so on.
- Build a small building with blocks or Legos in the center of the table.
- Make personalized block place mats out of construction paper.

## COSTUMES

- Cut out shapes from felt and pin them to babies' shirts with safety pins.

- Make square hats from large milk cartons covered with colorful contact paper.

## GAMES

- Building Block Races: Divide guests into two groups, and have them race to see who can make the tallest tower—before it tumbles over!
- Big Blocks Obstacle Course: Make blocks out of medium-sized cardboard boxes and paint them different colors or cover

them with wrapping paper. Set up an obstacle course and have babies climb over the blocks, go around them, crawl under them, and so on.
- Silly Stack: Collect a number of stackable items—anything from plastic food containers and canned foods to boxes of cereal and rolls of toilet paper. Have guests take turns stacking one on top of the other, until the stack falls!
- Build a Building: Collect a bunch of building blocks from neighbors and guests' parents and place them all in a big pile in the middle of the room. Let the babies build whatever they want with the blocks.

## ACTIVITIES

- Make and Guess: Have guests make "something" using construction materials. When they finish, have them try to guess what they built!
- Milk-Carton Blocks: Have guests make their own simple blocks out of milk cartons. Ask the parents to save milk cartons, clean them, and bring them to the

## BLOCK CAKE

1. Follow your favorite recipe to bake a square cake; cool.
2. Frost the cake with white frosting, and frost outside edges with a contrasting color.
3. Use petits fours to simulate blocks, and make a design or a building on top of the cake.

or

1. Cut the square cake into many smaller squares and freeze them so they are easier to frost.
2. Let guests decorate the squares with frosting and decorations.

or

1. Bake three square cakes; cool.
2. Cut one cake an inch smaller on all sides, and another cake an inch smaller than that, so you have three squares of different sizes.
3. Stack the squares on top of each other, the smallest at the top.
4. Frost each square a different color.

party. Collect the cartons, cut them to the size of a square, and insert one carton into another of the same size—open end to open end—to form a block. Let guests cover the milk-carton blocks with stickers, magazine cutouts, contact paper, and papier-mâché. Then let them play with the new blocks and take home their own.

- Build a Town: Ask parents to send along some of their kids' construction materials to share at the party. Place them all in the middle of the room and let the kids work together to create a whole town.
- Block Picture: Cut out shapes of different sizes and colors from

construction paper. Give each kid a large sheet of white paper and place the shapes on the table. Let the kids glue the shapes onto the paper to make designs, buildings, or anything they want.

## FOOD

- Cut out cookies from refrigerator dough, using cookie cutters in a variety of basic shapes. Let the kids frost the cookies before they eat them.
- Cut bread into squares, rectangles, triangles, and circles. Fill the sandwiches with a favorite filling.
- Cut cheese into small cubes and buy square crackers. Build a small tower from the cheese and crackers and serve to kids. Let them play with their food and build their own creations before they gobble them up.
- Make Carrot-and-Celery Constructions: Cut carrots into circles and cut celery into thin sticks. Set the rounds and sticks out on the table and have guests make flat designs on their plates. Then let them eat their construction materials. Provide dips.

## FAVORS

- Send the builders home with a small package of Legos, Duplos, blocks, or other construction and building toys.
- Give inexpensive books featuring different shapes.

## VARIATION

- Make building blocks by stuffing brown paper bags with crumpled newspapers, then tape the tops flat. Kids and parents can decorate the big blocks to look like buildings or anything they like. These blocks are light and large, and are therefore easy and safe for babies.

## HELPFUL HINTS

- Have appropriately sized materials so the younger babies don't swallow small pieces.
- Be sure to provide plenty of materials for each child, in case the children don't want to share.

# DOLLY'S TEA PARTY

Invite young guests' dollies to come to a tea party and share the fun with everyone. Make miniatures of everything so the dolls can participate in the fun.

## INVITATIONS

- Paper Dolls: Buy paper dolls and cut or punch them out. Write party details on the back of the doll. Be sure to ask the babies to bring their own dolls to the party.
- Tea Packet: Buy decorative herbal tea packets for the parents. Write party details on a small card and glue the card to the back of the tea packet.
- Picture Poses: Cut out pictures of dolls and tea sets from toy catalogs and glue them to the front of a folded sheet of pink paper to make a collage. Write party details inside.

## DECORATIONS

- Set small tables together in the middle of the room and cover with a tablecloth featuring toys or dolls. Set up small chairs around the table.

- Set dolls around the room and on the tables.
- Place tea sets or small plates and cups on the tables.
- Cut out paper dolls and pictures of dolls and tape them to the walls at a baby's eye level.

## COSTUMES

- Instruct guests to dress up in their very best clothes for a

fancy tea party, or dress like their doll, using colorful crepe paper to create matching outfits.

- Make fancy hats or buy them at a party or costume store to top each guest's outfit!

## GAMES

- Guess the Cookie: Break a variety of cookies into pieces and place the pieces of each cookie in separate paper cups. Have babies close their eyes, pick a cookie piece from a cup, taste it, and try to guess the cookie.
- What's Different about Dolly? Take each dolly out of the room for a moment and do something different to it, such as braid the hair, change the outfit, add some jewelry, remove shoes,

and so on. Bring the dolls back and have babies guess what's different about dolly!

- Crazy Table: Set up the table for the tea party and let the guests see the setup. Then have guests leave the party room for a few minutes. While they're gone, do crazy things to the table setting. (Turn a cup upside down, replace a plate with a coaster, turn the silverware upside down, and so on.) Have the guests come back in and try to find everything that's crazy!

## DOLLY CAKE

1. Bake a cake mix in an oven-proof bowl according to package directions. Turn out curved-side up and cool.
2. Insert a Barbie-type doll into the middle of the cake.
3. Use a frosting tube with a star tip to cover the bust of the doll and the whole cake with frosting to form a fancy dress.
4. Decorate with frosting tubes to add details.

## ACTIVITIES

- Decorating Cookies: Bake a batch of cookies, but leave them plain. Set them on the table together with frosting, frosting tubes, and candy decorations. Let guests decorate their own tea cookies. Or do the same with cupcakes and call them Tea Cakes.
- Dress Up Dolly: Provide a bunch of doll clothes and let guests dress up their dollies. Or provide

crepe paper or fabric remnants and let the babies design their own outfits for their dollies.

- Dress Up Baby: Provide a variety of fun, thrift-store dress-up clothes, such as hats, gloves, boots, high heels, sequin tops, velvet skirts or pants, and so on. Place them all in a big box and let the kids dress up.
- Picture Place Mats: Take a Polaroid photo of each child. Give each a paper doily. Have each child glue his photo in the center of his doily and decorate around the edges with felt-tip pens. Cover the place mats with clear contact paper to protect them and place them under the plates.

## FOOD

- After the kids have frosted their cookies, let them gobble them up.
- Give each guest a piece of white bread with the crusts removed. Pour food coloring into small bowls and hand out small paint-brushes. Have guests paint designs on the bread. When they finish, lightly toast the bread, cut each slice into fourths, and use them to make tea sandwiches with favorite fillings.
- Pour fruit-flavored herbal teas into the tiny cups and serve with slices of orange or sprigs of mint.

## FAVORS

- Hand out small, inexpensive dolls.
- Give guests toy tea sets and play food.

## VARIATIONS

- Have a special tea party in a banquet room at a local restaurant.

## HELPFUL HINTS

- Place a plastic tarp under the table to protect the floor, especially if the table is in a carpeted room.

# IT'S BEEN A BIG YEAR PARTY

This party features highlights from your baby's life over the past year and is a great family-and-friends party for the baby's first birthday. Watch time fly!

## INVITATIONS

- Baby's First Picture: Photocopy your baby's very first picture and use it as the front of a folded invitation. Inside, write the party details under the heading "Vital Statistics." Cut strips of white plastic to simulate hospital bands and write your baby's name and birth date on one side with a permanent felt-tip pen.
- Baby Birth Certificate: Make your own Baby Birth Certificate invitation using a computer. Find a real birth certificate to use as a model. Fill in some of your baby's vital statistics, then add the party's statistics. Print the certificate on parchment paper, roll into a scroll, and mail in a paper-towel tube painted pale pink or blue.

## DECORATIONS

- Select a number of pictures and mementos from your baby's past year. Tape them onto sheets of colored construction paper to frame them, then tape the pictures on the walls in chronological sequence (but without dates).
- Hang "It's a Boy/Girl" banner at the front door to greet the guests.

- Set your baby's favorite toys in the middle of the party table as a centerpiece.
- Play your baby's favorite music in the background.
- Create signs of your baby's milestones, such as First Tooth, First Haircut, First Day at Preschool, and so on.

## COSTUMES

- Dress your baby in her favorite outfit.

## GAMES

- How Well Do You Know Baby? Using the pictures and mementos on the wall, have the guests try to match them to specific dates. Do the same with your baby's milestones and see if they know when she took her first step, said her first word, or used the toilet. Ask trivia questions about your baby, such as, "How much did she weigh at birth?" "What's her middle name?" "Who was she named after?" "What time was she born?" and "Who's her doctor?"
- Guess Baby's Weight: Gently pass your baby from person to person and have each guess how much she weighs today. Put her on a scale and award a prize to the winner.
- Baby Can: Many people don't realize how much a baby can—and can't—do. Write a list of tasks your baby can do, such as "Touch her nose," "Eat with a spoon," "Put on her shoes," and "Turn on the VCR," and add some she can't do yet, such as "Brush her teeth," "Say the alphabet,"

"Dial the phone," and "Eat a carrot." Have guests try to guess the tasks your baby can do.

- Baby Food Tasting Game: Buy a variety of baby foods. Cover the jars to just above the labels with foil; remove the lids. Give each player a paper plate. Have guests place a glob of each food on their plates. When everyone is served, have each guest taste each glob and guess each food! Then unveil the labels to see whose taste buds are right!

## BIRTH CERTIFICATE CAKE

1. Bake a favorite sheet cake according to recipe directions; cool.
2. Cover the cake with white frosting.
3. Use frosting tubes to write basic vital statistics, such as your baby's name, parents' names, date and place of birth, and so on.
4. Decorate the cake with small baby toys, such as blocks, teethers, plastic dolls, rattles, and so on.

- Baby Gadgets: Get out some baby gadgets that most people are not likely to know, such as a bulb syringe, a heat-sensitive thermometer strip, a medication for swollen gums, a teether, and so on. Pass them around one by one, and have parents write down what they think it is or what it does. When all the objects have been identified, have the guests read their answers. Some of them should be funny! After all the guests read their guesses, share the real answers.

## ACTIVITIES

- Baby's Time Capsule: Have everyone bring something that

represents an important moment or significant relationship in your baby's life, such as a picture of a relative, a poem about her first step, a small toy she no longer plays with, or just a memory written down on paper. Seal the items in a container. Then set the container in a closet, bury it in the backyard, or place it in a safe deposit box—to be opened when your baby is twenty-one!

- Baby's Portrait: Pass out large sheets of white paper and drawing pens. Have everyone at the party draw a portrait of your baby. You should end up with some funny pictures to save in her scrapbook.

## FOOD

- Serve your baby's favorite foods at your party, such as minipizzas, spaghetti, cheese and crackers, applesauce, and so on. Serve everyone with baby-size plates and cups.
- Make sandwiches from bread tinted your baby's favorite color, or cut sandwiches into her favorite shapes using cookie cutters.

## FAVORS

- Hand out Baby-and-You Polaroids: Make small frames from cardboard and let the guests decorate the frames with wrapping paper, contact paper, stickers, or colored foil. Take a Polaroid photo of each guest holding your baby, and let each guest place the photo inside the frame to keep as a memento.

## VARIATIONS

- Have a professional photographer take a group picture of everyone, then individual pictures of all the guests with your baby.
- Have a joint It's Been a Big Year Party for several babies of the same age.

## HELPFUL HINTS

- Ask your guests to help with memories and mementos of your baby as you plan your It's Been a Big Year Party.

# KIDDIE CRAFTS PARTY

Kids begin developing their artistic ability at an early age. Give them a chance to craft their own creative fun—at a Kiddie Crafts Party!

## INVITATIONS

- Stencil Invitation: Cut out your own stencil or buy one from a craft shop. Fold a piece of white paper in half and stencil the design on the front. Write party information inside. Keep the design simple and include a package of crayons along with the invitation, so the invited guest can color the invitation as soon as he receives it.
- Magic Pens: Using an invisible-ink pen, draw a picture in the middle of a sheet of white paper. With a regular pen, write around the edge party details and instructions to color the middle of the paper with the enclosed pen. Enclose a pen that reveals the invisible drawing.

## DECORATIONS

- Set up a room just for arts and crafts; cover the floor with plastic

or newspapers. Or host the party outside.
- Provide easels, tables, and large sheets of white paper for creating artwork and crafts, along with lots of craft materials, such as markers, safety scissors, glue, fabric scraps, sequins, glitter, stickers, colored paper, and so on.
- Hang kids' art projects around the room at their eye level.

- Decorate the party table with art supplies.
- Make place mats to look like artists' palettes.

## COSTUMES

- Give the young guests smocks made from old white shirts (you can buy them cheaply at a thrift store) dotted with felt-tip pens and smeared with paint.

## GAMES

- Dough Designs: Give the kids Play-Doh or baker's clay (dough made with flour, salt, and water) and have them shape the material any way they like. When everyone finishes, have everyone guess what each dough object is supposed to be!
- Marble Painting: Give each guest a marble and a shoebox lid lined with a sheet of white construction paper. Set out bowls of liquid tempera paint and small plastic spoons. Have

the artists drop their marbles into a bowl of paint, retrieve them with the spoons, and carefully drop the marbles into the shoebox lids. Tell them to close their eyes and roll the marbles around so their paper can be covered with line designs. Then have them open their eyes and figure out what their design looks like!

## ACTIVITIES

• Finger-Paint with Pudding: This is a fun, safe, and tasty way to finger-paint. Prepare some chocolate and vanilla instant puddings according to package directions.

### PALETTE CAKE

1. Bake a round cake following a favorite recipe. Cool.
2. Frost the cake with white frosting.
3. Decorate the top of the cake to look like an artist's palette—use small candies or colored frosting to make circles of "paint." Set a clean new paintbrush on top of the cake.

Divide the vanilla pudding into parts and tint each a different color, using food coloring. Set bowls of pudding on a table covered with large sheets of slick paper. Have kids spoon a small amount of pudding onto the paper and finger-paint with it!

• Blow-a-Straw Painting: Give guests sheets of white paper and straws. Drop a small amount of watery paint at the bottom of each paper and have kids blow the paint upward with straws, spreading the paint on the paper. Try this with black paper and white paint for a different look.

- Decorate T-shirts: Give each baby a white T-shirt, or request on the invitations that they bring a white T-shirt that can be decorated. Cover an area of floor with thick cardboard from the sides of large boxes. Insert a thinner, smaller piece of cardboard inside each T-shirt (this will keep paint from running through to the back). Tack the shirt and thin cardboard down to the heavier cardboard, keeping the front surface flat. Have kids decorate their T-shirts with puffy paints. Allow the T-shirts to dry and let guests wear the shirts home at the end of the party.

## FOOD

- After the painters finish finger-painting with pudding, serve them fresh bowls of chocolate and vanilla pudding to eat!
- Bake or buy large cookies and let the guests decorate them any way they want, using tubes of icing, gels, and sprinkles.
- Make Patchwork Sandwiches: Ask the bakery to tint bread four colors: pink, blue, yellow, and green. Make sandwiches with the colored bread, then cut them into triangles. Arrange the triangles on a platter in a patchwork design.

## FAVORS

- Hand out craft supplies, such as markers, stickers, glitter, glue, safety scissors, construction paper, Popsicle sticks, and so on. Gather the materials in small decorated boxes.
- Let the young artists keep their decorated T-shirts.
- Make extra baker's clay and give each guest a portion to take home.

## VARIATIONS

- Invite an arts-and-crafts teacher to lead the group in some creative activities.

## HELPFUL HINTS

- Use safe, nontoxic, age-appropriate materials.
- Protect your party room from spills.

# KINDER-GYM PARTY

A good workout at a Kinder-Gym Party makes a great time for babies. You provide the equipment; the kids will provide the energy and muscle!

## INVITATIONS

- Exercise Headbands: Make headbands from stretchy fabric, or buy inexpensive ones that fit around babies' foreheads. Write party details on the headbands using a felt-tip pen.
- Baby Barbells: Cut out barbell shapes from black construction paper. Glue large pompoms on the ends to make the barbells look three-dimensional. Write party details on the back using white-ink pens.

## DECORATIONS

- Set up Kinder-Gym in the party room, where all the action will take place:
  - Spread exercise mats or blankets on the floor to cushion the workout. Add mattresses and pillows if you like.
  - Set out exercise equipment, spaced far enough apart so the guests have plenty of room to move around. You might include a variety of large balls, several pillows, a wide balance beam, an obstacle course, a tunnel (a cardboard box or two, taped together), a climbing apparatus, Hula-Hoops, jump ropes, and heavy toys to lift.

—Hang up posters of babies and/or pictures of exercise equipment cut from toy catalogs.

—Play baby exercise music in the background.

## COSTUMES

- Have the athletes wear the headbands from the invitations, or provide extra headbands at the party.
- Ask everyone to wear comfortable clothing.

## GAMES

- Rollover Ball: Have each baby stand on one side of a large ball and have a parent stand on the other side. Stretch the baby over the ball and roll the ball toward the parent, so the baby's feet come off the ground. Repeat, rolling farther each time.

- Pull-Me-Ups: Help the guests sit on the floor by a couch. Have them try to pull themselves up onto the couch with parents' encouragement.
- Creep and Crawl: Line guests up at one end of the room and line parents up at the other end. At the word "Go!" have the babies and toddlers hurry across the room to reach their parents. Whoever arrives first wins the race.

## BABY BARBELL CAKE

1. Bake two round cakes following a favorite recipe. Cool.
2. Cover both cakes with chocolate frosting.
3. Set the two cakes a few inches apart and connect them with a row of rectangular cookies to make the barbell shape.
4. Top the two cakes with miniature plastic babies.

- Obstacle Course: Set up an age-appropriate obstacle course. You might have the babies crawl over a pillow, creep under a blanket, crawl through a box, climb over a cushion, and so on.
- Somersault Stunts: Teach the young guests how to do a somersault, then see who can somersault across the room.
- Chase Me: Select one parent to be the chaser, and have that person chase the kids all around the room. Anyone who gets caught gets to sit on the

couch, cheer the other players, and wait for the others to be caught, too.

## ACTIVITIES

- Warm-Up Massage: Before exercising, warm up the guests with a gentle massage. Spread lotion on their bodies (which are dressed only in diapers or underpants).
- Cool-Down Massage: After exercising, lay the babies down on the blankets and give them a soothing cool-down massage, to help relax and calm them.

## FOOD

- Make Busy Body Bites out of refrigerator biscuit dough, bake, and serve with jam to hungry babies and toddlers.
- If the babies are old enough to eat carrot sticks, make dumbbells by sticking balls of soft cheese on the ends of carrot sticks.
- Serve lots of fruit juices, water, or milk in squirt bottles for fun. Or make fruit-and-milk smoothies in a blender.

## FAVORS

- Give different-sized balls to take home.
- Hand out exercise accessories, such as headbands, wristbands, sport socks, T-shirts with stripes or numbers, towels, and water bottles.

## VARIATIONS

- Take the kids to a real baby gym class for an hour of fun and exercise.

## HELPFUL HINTS

- Ask parents to help out at the party, so all the babies get lots of personal attention and assistance.
- Avoid being too competitive with the games. It doesn't matter who wins, so award everyone a prize.
- Spot babies at all times to make sure they don't hurt themselves.

# MOTHER GOOSE PARTY

A Mother Goose Party is a fairy tale come true for babies. Most will be familiar with the rhymes and characters and will love to listen and sing along.

## INVITATIONS

- Mother Goose Books: Cut out a picture from an inexpensive Mother Goose book and glue it to the front of a folded piece of colored construction paper. Inside, write the party information in story form, such as "Once upon a time, there was a Mother Goose Party. . . ." Include extra pages if you like—blank or with personalized rhymes.

## DECORATIONS

- Draw reproductions of some Mother Goose characters on large sheets of white paper. Or you might buy large, inexpensive picture books and cut out the pages. Tape the characters or pages to the walls at a baby's eye level.
- For the Pumpkin Eater, set up a pumpkin on the table as a centerpiece.
- For Little Miss Muffet, cut spiderweb place mats from construction paper and hang plastic spiders from the ceiling.
- Set out stuffed animals and dolls that resemble Mother Goose characters.
- Play Mother Goose songs and rhymes in the background.

## COSTUMES

- Offer accessories that correspond to various Mother Goose rhymes: nightshirts and/or nightcaps ("Willie Winkie"), chef's hats ("Pat-a-Cake"), shepherd's

staff and sheep's tails ("Little Bo-Peep"), bells for shoes ("Ride a Cock-Horse"), and so on.

## GAMES

- Free the Pumpkin Eater's Wife: Have guests form a circle by holding hands to make the pumpkin shell. Place a player in the center of the circle to be the wife, who is trapped inside. The wife must try to get out of the shell by ducking under the players' arms without breaking the pumpkin (the connected hands). Have the circle of players chant "Peter, Peter, Pumpkin Eater, had a wife and couldn't keep her. Put her in a pumpkin shell, and there he kept her very well."

- Jack Be Nimble Jump-Over: Cover a quart-sized milk carton or an empty Pringles container with white paper to make a "candlestick." Cover the top of the carton with red paper to make a flame. Have the kids jump over the "stick" one by one, trying not to get "burned" (by knocking over the carton).

- Spider Scare: Hide a plastic spider in the room and have guests search for it so Little Miss Muffet won't get scared. The guest who finds the spider wins a prize. (Make sure the spider is pretty easy to find.)

- Crooked Walk: Lay a long length of rope down on the floor in a twisting, zigzag design. Have the kids walk along the rope from one end to the other without "falling off" the crooked walk. Have them recite the rhyme: "There was a crooked man who went a crooked mile. He found a crooked sixpence against a crooked stile. He bought a crooked cat, which caught a crooked mouse, and they all lived together in a little crooked house."

- Ride a Cock-Horse: Attach bells to guests' shoes and have them pretend to ride horses and make noise with the bells.
- Little Bo-Peep: Have each guest take a turn being Little Bo-Peep, who runs after the sheep (the rest of the guests on all fours) and tries to catch them! Or make tails out of construction paper, attach double-sided tape to the

top of the tail, and have Bo-Peep try to stick the tail on the run-away sheep (again, the guests)!

## STORYBOOK CAKE

1. Bake a sheet cake following a favorite recipe. Cool.
2. Cut the cake in half and cover both halves with white frosting.
3. Set the cakes next to each other to form an open book.
4. Write "Happy Birthday" or a Mother Goose rhyme on the "pages."
5. Set Mother Goose characters on top or around the bottom of the cake.

## ACTIVITIES

- Three Blind Mice: Blindfold the kids one at a time and see if they can find the hidden "cheese" in the party room. Hide the cheese creatively, such as partially under a cushion or on top of a low shelf, but keep it in plain sight. Make the cheese out of a large triangular piece of Styrofoam painted gold, yellow, or orange.
- London Bridge: Have two guests face each other, join hands, and raise their arms high to form a

bridge. Tell the other guests to pass under the bridge and sing the song "London Bridge Is Falling Down." When they come to the line "all fall down," whoever is under the bridge is captured (by lowered arms) and out of the game. Continue playing until only one player remains.

- Ring around the Rosie: Have guests join hands and form a circle, then tell them to sing "Ring around the Rosie" and fall down at the appropriate time.

## FOOD

- Make Jell-O Goosey Gander's Eggs: Mix Jell-O according to package directions. Pour the mixture into plastic eggs and let the eggs set in the refrigerator until firm. Discard plastic eggs and place the Jell-O eggs in a bowl on the table.
- Fill party bags with nursery-rhyme-related goodies, such as gummy mice for "Three Blind Mice," Goldfish crackers for "Three Little Fishes," veggies for "Mary, Mary, Quite Contrary," pumpkin seeds for "Peter the Pumpkin Eater," muffins for "The Muffin Man," and so on.
- Serve Queen's Tarts: Roll out sugar-cookie dough and cut into heart shapes. Cut a small heart out of the center of half the cookies. Bake according to package directions. When cool, spread the whole cookies with jam, then top with cookies that have hearts cut out in the center. Pass out to knaves.

## FAVORS

- Hand out Mother Goose books to be enjoyed at home.
- Give toys based on Mother Goose characters.
- Provide Mother Goose rhymes on tape.

## VARIATION

- Rent a Mother Goose storytelling video from the library.

## HELPFUL HINTS

- Before playing each game, read aloud the rhyme upon which the game is based.
- Check out Mother Goose books from a library for more ideas.

# MUSIC MAKER PARTY

Babies are natural music makers. Just tune up a party and listen to the sounds of fun!

## INVITATIONS

- Listening Invitation: Buy inexpensive audiotapes, one for each guest. Sing your invitation, accompanied by some appropriate music, and record it on tape. Then copy the tape for each guest.
- Music Note: Cut out large music notes from black construction paper and write party details with white ink.
- Score Sheets: Buy blank music score sheets and write party details up and down the lines to look like lines of music.

## DECORATIONS

- Cut out giant black music notes from construction paper and tape them to the walls at a baby's eye level.
- Hang a few music notes from the ceiling to dance above guests' heads.

- Hang up posters of child singing stars, such as Mary-Kate and Ashley Olsen.
- Create a table centerpiece out of toy musical instruments.
- Cover the table with white paper and draw lines on it to look like sheet music.
- Make place mats out of music notes and write the guests' names in the centers.
- Play children's music in the background.

## COSTUMES

- Dress guests in T-shirts decorated with music notes.
- Have guests wear elastic bracelets and/or anklets with bells securely attached.

## GAMES

- Musical Chairs: Play the classic game of Musical Chairs with a twist. Set up chairs—enough for all but one guest—in a circle or row. March the kids around the chairs while you play music. When the music stops, guests must rush to find a chair. The player without a chair is out of the game —but she gets a prize anyway!
- Name That Tot Tune: Prerecord five to ten seconds of familiar children's songs on tape. Have guests gather in a circle. Play the first song segment, then stop the tape and let guests guess the song.
- What's That Sound? Tape-record a variety of familiar sounds from around the home or neighborhood. You might include the sound of a barking dog, an alarm clock, a flushing toilet, a car horn, a vacuum, a doorbell, a telephone ringing, a noisy toy, and so on. Play the tape, one sound at a time, and let the kids guess each sound.
- Make Up a Song: Seat everyone in a circle. Play a simple instrument, such as a guitar or ukulele, and go around the circle making up lines to a song, beginning with the guest to your right. To get the composers started, make up the first line yourself.

## ACTIVITIES

- Homemade Concert: Create your own musical instruments together (use books from a library or bookstore for ideas). You can make drums from oatmeal boxes, kazoos from toilet-paper rolls

## DRUM CAKE

1. Bake a double-layer round cake following a favorite recipe. Cool.
2. Frost the top of one layer and set the other layer on top; frost the sides of the cake, leaving an inch from the top unfrosted all around.
3. Frost the top of the cake and the unfrosted inch on the sides with a different color.
4. Use frosting tubes to make a zigzag design on the side of the cake.
5. Set two bread sticks crisscrossed on the top of the cake to make drumsticks.
6. Place tiny toy musical instruments around the bottom of the cake or on top of the drum.

covered at one end with wax paper, shakers from small plastic containers filled with seeds or sand, tambourines from stiff paper plates glued together with bells inside or tongue depressors with jingle bells hot-glued on the ends, and simple noisemakers from smooth wooden blocks. Then put in earplugs and put on a concert!

- Musical Parade: Give each guest a homemade or inexpensive toy musical instrument and stage a musical parade around the house or the neighborhood.

- Sing-Along: Play guests' favorite music and have them sing along.

## FOOD
- Create Piano Sandwiches using white and brown bread with crusts removed. Fill the sandwiches with peanut butter and jelly, cut into thin rectangles, and line up alternating brown and white rectangles to resemble piano keys.
- Serve Musical Milk: Pour milk into clear plastic glasses, filling only halfway. Give straws to the guests and let them blow bubbles into the milk while humming tunes, as though they are "playing" the milk! Or fill the glasses with varying amounts of milk and let guests tap the sides of the glasses to make music.
- Serve "noisy" foods, such as crunchy celery and carrot sticks, crackers and chips, popcorn, and so on.
- Make cookies shaped like musical notes using a cookie cutter, if available, or shape the cookies freehand using a sharp knife. Decorate cookies with small candies or frosting. Serve lined up on the sheet-music tablecloth. (See Decorations.)

## FAVORS
- Hand out kazoos, harmonicas, and other inexpensive toy musical instruments.
- Give sing-along tapes of favorite tunes.

## VARIATIONS
- Have a baby dance party. Just turn on the music and let guests dance up a storm. Teach them a few simple steps when they get tired of making up their own.
- Play music videos, such as *Barney Sings* or *Sesame Street Tunes*.

## HELPFUL HINTS
- This is a noisy party, so provide your grown-up guests with earplugs! Warn your neighbors so they know what is going on.

# PARTY ON SESAME STREET

Sunny day! Everything's A-okay at your Party on Sesame Street. Invite Big Bird, Bert and Ernie, and Cookie Monster to join the fun!

## INVITATIONS

- Big Bird: Fold a piece of construction paper in half to make a card. Cut out a picture of Big Bird from a magazine or an inexpensive children's book and glue it to the front of the card. Glue bright yellow feathers onto Big Bird to make him three-dimensional. Write party details inside the card.
- Sesame Street Sign: Draw Sesame Street signs on construction paper. Draw a map from each guest's house to your Party on Sesame Street. Mark Sesame Street characters' homes along the way.
- The Count Counts: Fold a piece of construction paper in half to make a card. Cut out a picture of the Count from a magazine or an inexpensive children's book and glue it to the front of the

card. Draw the Count's fingers to match the age of the birthday baby. Write party details inside the card.

## DECORATIONS

- Make a Sesame Street sign for the lawn or front door.
- Place a large poster of your favorite Sesame Street character at the door to greet guests as they arrive, or have a parent dress in costume and open the door to surprise guests.

- Inside the party room, set out Sesame Street characters and hang posters of the characters on the wall at a baby's eye level.
- Set up Oscar's garbage can, Cookie Monster's cookie table, and other special places for your favorite characters.
- Set the table using Sesame Street party products (available at party stores).
- Create a centerpiece using Sesame Street characters.
- Play Sesame Street tunes.

## COSTUMES

- Using face paints, decorate guests' faces with the colors of their favorite Sesame Street characters—yellow for Big Bird, blue for Grover or Cookie Monster, green for Oscar the Grouch or Kermit the Frog.
- Make Big Bird headbands with large yellow feathers sticking out.
- Have guests wear Count capes.

## GAMES

- Big Bird's Winding Walk: Cut out Big Bird's footprints from yellow or orange construction paper and set up a winding path for guests to follow. Have guests walk all over the house, the yard, and the neighborhood stepping on the prints as they go.
- Grover's Getcha Game: Tie a Grover doll to a rope and set him in the middle of the party room. Have one of the guests try to get Grover when you say, "Go!" Every time he or she tries to get Grover, pull the rope so he jumps out of reach. Continue until the player finally catches Grover. Repeat for all players.

- Kermit Jumps and Hops and Skips: Choose one player to be Kermit. Have the rest of the guests get in line behind Kermit. Have Kermit move around the room, changing his movements from jumping to hopping to skipping and so on. The other players must follow everything Kermit does. Have guests take turns being Kermit.

## ACTIVITIES

- Sesame Street Stick Puppets: Buy inexpensive Sesame Street picture books and cut out the

characters. Have guests sit at a table. Hand out several tongue depressors to each guest. Let the kids pick a few characters and glue them onto their sticks to make Sesame Street Stick Puppets. Then put on a show (see next activity).

- Sesame Street Puppet Show: After the kids make their Stick Puppets, it's time to make a puppet theater. Before the party, get a large appliance box. Cut out the top half of one side, to make the stage opening, and cut out the bottom half of the opposite side so the kids can climb in with their puppets. Staple a piece of fabric on the

### BERT AND ERNIE CAKES

1. Bake two round cakes following a favorite recipe. Cool.
2. Cover one cake with yellow frosting and one with orange frosting.
3. Set the cakes side by side on platters. Decorate one to look like Bert and one to look like Ernie, copying pictures from a Sesame Street book.
4. Add Sesame Street figures around the bottom of the cakes.

inside of the stage opening, across the top, so the audience can't see inside the box (the fabric will also serve as a curtainlike backdrop when the puppets come up from below). Cut out street scenes from inexpensive Sesame Street books, such as street signs, trees, houses, lampposts, and so on. Glue them all over the front of the box to set the stage. Have a couple of kids get inside the box with their puppets and put on a show. Take turns giving shows.

- Story Hour: Read a favorite Sesame Street story, such as *The Monster at the End of This Book.* As you read, have guests act out the story with their puppets.

## FOOD

- Since *Sesame Street* teaches about shapes, make a variety of sandwiches and cut them into the four basic shapes: squares, rectangles, circles, and triangles. Set the Shape Sandwiches on a platter and let guests pick the shapes they want. Have them try to make something with the shapes before they eat them.

- Make Big Bird's favorite birdseed trail mix: Fill individual sandwich baggies with a variety of seeds, chopped nuts, cereals, and dried fruit. Tie baggies with yellow ribbons.

- Serve a Monster Cookie: Roll out refrigerator sugar-cookie dough into one giant monster of a cookie. Bake a little longer than instructed, until golden brown around the edges. Let guests decorate the cookie with frosting and candy sprinkles.

## FAVORS

- Hand out small Sesame Street toys, dolls, and figures.
- Offer Sesame Street coloring books, picture books, and sing-along tapes.

## VARIATION

- Watch a tape of *Sesame Street* or rent a Muppet movie.

## HELPFUL HINT

- Hire a costumed character to come to the party for a special treat, or rent a costume yourself for fun.

# PUPPET PARTY

Bring the magic of make-believe to life with a Puppet Party! All you need are some basic supplies to create your new party friends!

## INVITATIONS
- Paper Bag Puppets: Buy pastel or brown lunch bags. Lay a bag flat, bottom side up. Draw eyes and a nose on the bottom flap, the upper part of a mouth at the edge of the flap, and the rest of the mouth continuing on the side of the paper bag, so the "mouth" opens when a hand is inserted inside the flap. Under the flap draw a tongue and teeth. Add hair to the top of the puppet's head using a felt-tip pen or yarn. Write party details inside the mouth or on the back.

## DECORATIONS
- Make a bunch of Paper Bag Puppets (see Invitations) and give each one a funny name. Or make the puppets resemble the guests and label each accordingly. Tape the puppets to the walls at a baby's eye level.

- Decorate the rest of the party room with a variety of puppets.
- Set up a miniature puppet show on the table to serve as a centerpiece; use a small cardboard box for the theater, and pop-up stick or finger puppets for the characters.
- Set up a puppet theater in the middle of the room. Paint a large appliance box with a bright color. Cut a horizontal rectangle in the front to use as a stage,

eyebrows, long lashes, pink circle cheeks, and big red lips.

## GAMES

- Guess the Puppet: Place familiar puppets in paper bags and close the bags. Have guests sit in a circle. Pass around one bag and ask guests to feel inside and try to guess the puppet inside. After everyone guesses, take out the puppet to see who is right! Continue with the other puppets.
- Pass the Puppet: Have guests sit in a circle. Play a story in the background and pass a puppet around the circle. After a few seconds, shut off the story. Whoever holds the puppet is out of the game. Continue until only one player remains.
- Faster Finger Plays: Decorate guests' fingers with funny faces using felt-tip pens, or buy small finger puppets. Teach guests a finger play involving the puppets. After guests learn the finger play, have them follow along. Repeat faster each time, until they give up!

and cut out the bottom half of the back of the box for the kids to enter and exit. Staple fabric across the stage opening, cut the fabric vertically in the center, and tie each side back with a twist tie. Note: As a party activity, have guests decorate the theater. (See Activities.)

## COSTUMES

- Use face paints to make guests look like puppets: Create dark

- Puppet Says: Give each child a puppet and hold a puppet yourself. Have the kids sit facing you, then lead them in a game of Puppet Says. Slowly call out simple commands, such as "Puppet says, 'Raise your arms.'" The kids must follow the instructions using their puppets. Try to trick the players by saying one thing but having your puppet do something else. Any player who follows Puppet's actions instead of Puppet's words is out of the game. Continue until only one player remains. Be sure to keep the commands simple and the movements slow so the kids can keep up and not get confused.

## PUPPET SHOW CAKE

1. Bake a sheet cake following a favorite recipe. Cool.
2. Cover the cake with white frosting.
3. Outline the edges of the cake with chocolate frosting to make it look like a box.
4. Outline a rectangle at the top of the cake to make a stage.
5. Set small finger puppets in the stage to make performers, and set several around the bottom of the cake to form an audience.

## ACTIVITIES

- Paper Bag Puppets: Have guests make their own Paper Bag Puppets (see Invitations). Provide paper bags, felt-tip pens, cloth scraps, glitter, glue, yarn for hair, large wiggly eyes, and other craft materials.
- Glove Puppets: Give guests one garden glove each and let them

decorate each finger with permanent felt-tip pens to make animals, creatures, family members, or whatever they like. Have them slip on their Glove Puppets and play!

- Decorate a Puppet Theater: Let guests decorate the puppet theater you've made as a decoration (see Decorations) with paint, felt-tip pens, crayons, stickers, or contact paper.
- Puppet Show! After making all the puppets and the theater, it's showtime. Choose two kids to be the puppeteers, and have the rest of the group be the audience. Let the puppeteers put on their show for five minutes, then choose two new kids to be the puppeteers. Continue rotating puppeteers and audience until everyone has had a turn. Videotape the shows and play them back at the end of showtime.

## FOOD

- Create Puppet Face Sandwiches: Cut bread into large circles and fill slices with a favorite filling. Cut up pieces of fruit and veggies. Let guests make their own Puppet Faces by decorating the tops of the bread slices with the cut-up pieces.
- Make Hand-Shaped Cookies: Roll out refrigerator cookie dough and use a hand-shaped cookie cutter to cut out cookies. Bake and cool. Print each guest's name on a left hand and a right hand, so each guest will have two cookies.

## FAVORS

- Send the puppeteers home with the puppets they've made.
- Hand out store-bought cloth puppets and finger puppets.
- Give books with finger plays for puppet play.

## VARIATION

- Hire a professional puppeteer to entertain the kids at the party.

## HELPFUL HINT

- When using materials for making puppets, be sure all decorations are attached securely and nothing is small enough for babies to swallow.

# STORYBOOK PARTY

Watch the characters from your child's favorite story step out of the book and into a Storybook Party! This party uses some popular children's stories, but you can choose any of your child's favorites.

## INVITATIONS

- Storybook Invitations: Cut a rectangle from colored construction paper and fold it half, making the front and back covers of a book. Write the name of the story on the front cover—if you like, personalize the title, such as "The Three Little Pigs and You." Fold rectangles of white paper and insert into the folded cover, making pages. Write party details worded as the story. Illustrate the book yourself, or cut up an inexpensive storybook and glue the pictures on the cover and inside. Staple the pages and the cover together and mail to guests.

## DECORATIONS

- Buy inexpensive storybooks and cut out pictures of the characters. Tape them to the walls at a baby's eye level in a storyboard setup, connecting all the characters to one another with speech balloons.
- Set out picture books featuring favorite stories, and dolls and animals from various storybooks.
- Photocopy book covers and use them as place mats.
- Form a table centerpiece using storybooks, dolls, and animals.

## COSTUMES

- Offer guests accessories from various storybooks: red hood and cape *(Little Red Riding Hood)*, pig snouts and wolf ears *(The Three Little Pigs)*, goat horns *(The Three Billy Goats Gruff)*, and so on.

## GAMES

- Find the Three Little Pigs: Hide three pig dolls or pictures cut from the storybook in the party room. Ask guests to find the pigs before the wolf comes! Have another adult make wolf sounds from another room to keep the suspense high and the action moving!
- Follow Red Riding Hood's Path: Create a path from cut-out wolf prints for Red Riding Hood to follow throughout the party house or in the backyard. The prints should lead to Grandma's bed. Along the path place little items from Red Riding Hood's basket, such as snacks, candies, or flowers. Give guests small baskets to collect the goodies as they find them. When they reach Grandma's bed, have them pull down the covers to find their prizes.
- Tramp over Billy Goat Bridge: Have a troll (an adult helper) lie face down on the floor. Cover the troll with pillows to make a bridge. Have guests climb over the bridge before the troll wakes up and

catches them. (Tell the troll to pretend to wake up once in a while to keep the game lively.)

## STORYBOOK CAKE

1. Bake a sheet cake following a favorite recipe. Cool.
2. Cover the top and one side of the cake with a colored frosting, then cover the remaining three sides with white frosting. Line the bottom edge of each white side with a thin strip of colored frosting. Your cake should now look like a closed book with a colored cover and white pages.
3. Draw thin horizontal lines with dark frosting on the white sides of the cake to emphasize the pages of the book.
4. Write the name of the birthday baby on top as the title of the book (for example, "Liya's Story").
5. Add a few groupings of small plastic storybook figures to the cake for detail.

## ACTIVITIES

- Storybook Play: Make a storybook come to life. Dress guests in costumes and accessories, and create any props appropriate for the story. Then read the book aloud and have the children act it out as you read.
- Storyteller: Hire a professional storyteller to come to the party. Or rent a costume appropriate to one of the stories and perform the story for the kids.

- Make-a-Story: Have the kids make up their own story. Have everyone sit in a circle. Begin a story yourself, then have the next player tell the next part of the story, and so on around the room.

## FOOD

- Serve Three Little Pigs in a Blanket: Unroll refrigerator biscuits, lay a cocktail wiener on top of each, and roll into biscuits. Bake according to directions on container, until lightly browned. Serve with mustard and ketchup.
- Make Little Red Riding Hood Goodie Baskets: Fill small baskets with finger foods, such as packages of some of the following: cut-up vegetables, pieces of fruit, crackers, small cheeses, chips, tiny sandwiches, and cookies.
- Make Hansel and Gretel Houses: Spread frosting on the sides of clean, empty, individual-sized milk cartons. Press graham crackers to the frosted sides. Spread frosting on the tops of the cartons and let the kids press cookies into the frosting to make roofs. Let kids decorate their cookie houses with frosting, raisins, and candies such as gumdrops and jelly beans.

## FAVORS

- Hand out popular storybooks.
- Give small toy figures of story-book characters.
- Let guests have some costume parts and props used in the storybook play.

## VARIATIONS

- If you like, design your party around only one particular story. For example, if you choose *The Three Little Pigs,* you can build a house, run from the Big Bad Wolf, sing "Who's Afraid of the Big, Bad Wolf?" and have a pig-shaped cake.
- Visit your local library's story-time.

## HELPFUL HINT

- For ideas for your storybook party, check out books from a library.

# TEDDY BEAR PICNIC

Invite your baby's favorite friends—live and stuffed—to a party and have a Teddy Bear Picnic in the party room or in the backyard!

## INVITATIONS

- Paper Teddy Bears: Cut out paper teddy bears from brown construction paper. Add face details with a black felt-tip pen. Write party details on the back. Attach song lyrics to "Teddy Bear's Picnic." Wrap the invitation in a bandanna before placing into an envelope. Address invitations to the kids and their teddy bears.

## DECORATIONS

- Cut out giant bears from large sheets of brown paper and tape them to the walls (or fence, if outside) at a baby's eye level.
- Cut out trees from brown and green construction paper and place them between the bears.
- Set out a large red-and-white-checked tablecloth on the floor or the ground for the picnic.
- Sprinkle plastic ants on the tablecloth.
- Set a teddy bear in a small picnic basket and place it in the middle of the tablecloth for a centerpiece.

## COSTUMES

- Give guests bear-ear headbands to wear when they arrive.
- Offer bibs to both guests and their bears. (See Activities.)

## GAMES

- Feel Fuzzy Bear: As each child arrives with a teddy bear, have the child put the bear in a large paper bag. Give the bag a number. Have all the guests sit in a circle. Pass around one of the bags and have guests feel the bear inside, without peeking. After all the bears have been passed around, have each child guess which bag holds her bear.

- Where's Teddy? After the guests arrive, take their teddy bears and hide them in another room. Then bring the kids into the room and let them search for their own bears. Tell them not to remove anyone else's bear or tell anyone where other bears are hiding.

- Do the Bear Crawl: Set up an obstacle course with objects to crawl over, through, around, underneath, and so on. Have guests follow the obstacle course on all fours, pretending they are bears.

- Bear Thief: Seat guests in a circle and have them put their bears behind their backs. Choose one player to be the thief. The thief walks around the outside of the circle for a few seconds, then grabs a bear. The person who owns that bear must get up and chase the thief to get the bear back. If she doesn't get her bear, she becomes the thief. If she does get her bear, she gets to sit down again with her bear safe in her lap.

## ACTIVITIES

- Teddy Bear Picnic: Have an indoor or outdoor picnic. Spread a tablecloth over the floor or ground and have guests sit on the cloth with their bears. Serve picnic foods from a large picnic basket or small individual baskets. Let guests serve their bears, too.

- Teddy Bear Bibs: Buy inexpensive white bibs for guests and their bears. Use brown felt-tip pens to draw teddy bears on guests' bibs. Let guests draw their own teddy bears on the bears' bibs. Encourage everyone—guests and bears—to wear their bibs.

- Bear Faces: Use face paints to turn guests into bears. Hold

### TEDDY BEAR CUPCAKES

1. Bake chocolate cupcakes following a favorite recipe. Cool.
2. Cover all cupcakes with chocolate frosting.
3. Make teddy bear faces using cherries for noses, raisins for eyes, licorice for mouths, and small round cookies for ears.

mirrors for the children so they can see their new bear faces. Be sure to take Polaroid photos of the painted children holding their stuffed bears.

## FOOD

- Mix up some portable bear food: Combine chopped nuts, cereals, dried fruit, coconut, and seeds in a bowl, then place in individual baggies for easy eating.
- Serve Honeycomb cereal with milk for a beary good snack. Offer a side of honey graham crackers or biscuits with jam.
- Make Bear-Faced Sandwiches: Cut sandwich bread into large circles for bear faces. Fill with a favorite filling. Cut maraschino cherries in half for bear noses, use raisins for eyes, and make mouths with thin strips of licorice. Serve to hungry kids and their teddy bears.
- Create Berry Bear Drinks with fresh or frozen strawberries. Place one cup of strawberries (cut-up fresh or thawed frozen) in a blender with five or six ice cubes. Add one cup milk, whirl until smooth, and serve. Makes two or three servings.

## FAVORS

- Give guests small bears to take home.
- Hand out picture books featuring teddy bears.
- Fill small plastic honey pots with teddy bear cookies, crackers, or gummy bears.

## VARIATION

- Take guests and their teddy bears on a trip to the zoo. Eat a picnic on the lawn and take a nature walk to see real bears. Be sure to have several adults along to help keep track of the children and their stuffed friends.

## HELPFUL HINTS

- Treat babies' bears carefully —they're very important guests.
- If a child doesn't have a teddy bear, have a few on hand to share.

# TRAINS, PLANES, AND AUTOMOBILES PARTY

As soon as baby starts moving, he wants to GO! Celebrate your baby's fascination with transportation with a Trains, Planes, and Automobiles party!

## INVITATIONS

- Wheels on a Car: Fold construction paper to make a card. Draw or glue a picture of a car on the front of the card. Cut out two circles from a different-colored construction paper to make wheels; attach them to the car using T-fasteners so the wheels can turn. Write party details inside. If you prefer, do the same for a train picture, or make propellers for a plane.
- Paper Airplane: Fold a sheet of colored construction paper into an airplane. Unfold, write party details inside, refold, and mail in a large envelope.

## DECORATIONS

- Decorate the party room to resemble an airport, train station, or gas station, or use all three motifs:
  - For an airport, lay out a long bedsheet or strip of butcher paper for a runway and set up chairs to look like the inside of a plane. (Do the same for a train or bus, using the sheet or paper as a road.)
  - For a plane or train, cut out two sides of a large cardboard box to make an entrance. Paint the

windows so they can look out. Paint the boxes inside and out, adding details like headlights, wheels, wipers, and so on.
–Create a gas station using cardboard boxes.

## COSTUMES

- Offer children engineer or pilot caps. Or buy small airplane pins or engineer bandannas.

## GAMES

- Race Cars: For each child, cut out the top and bottom of a large box, leaving only the sides. Have children step into their cars, pull them up to their waists, and run a race.
- Bus Pass: Have everyone sit in two single-file lines. Give each line leader a plate of cotton balls to pass back over his head. The players must try not to spill any cotton as they race to get the plate to the last player in their line. Repeat the game with a variety of challenges, such as passing a cup of water, putting on and taking off an article of clothing, and so on.

inside and outside of the box with appropriate details.
–For a bus, lay a large appliance box on its side, cut off the top so kids can sit inside, and cut out windows along both sides. Paint the box yellow and add details inside and out.
–For cars, get a large box for each guest, cut off the tops of the boxes so kids can sit inside them, and cut out

- Sounds of Transportation: Find a children's tape that plays a variety of transportation sounds, such as a car engine, a bus horn, a motorcycle, a plane engine, or a train crossing—or tape the sounds yourself. Play the tape and have children guess the sounds.

## ACTIVITIES

- Make a Car: Let guests design their own cars. Provide individual cardboard boxes, cut and ready to go, then let guests paint their cars and decorate

**CHOO-CHOO CAKE**

1. Bake a sheet cake following a favorite recipe. Cool.
2. Cut the cake into small rectangles and set the rectangles end to end to make train cars. Make one train car per guest, if possible.
3. Frost each train car with different-colored frosting.
4. Add details with small candies, strings of licorice, frosting tubes, and other decorative items.

them with markers and stickers, adding headlights, doors, windows, and so on. Provide some fun accessories to add, such as bumper stickers, reflector tape, bike horns, antenna balls, and so on. Have a car parade down the sidewalk when you're finished.

- Pilot/Engineer: Invite an airline pilot or train engineer to the party. Ask the pilot to come in uniform and talk about what it's like to fly a plane or drive a train.
- Storytime: Read stories that feature trains (*The Little Engine That Could*), planes (*The Big*

*Book of Airplanes),* or other modes of transportation. Sing "The Wheels on the Bus Go Round and Round," then make up your own lyrics for planes, trains, and automobiles.

## FOOD

- Make sandwiches with kids' favorite fillings: Cut off crusts and cut sandwiches in half. Lay sandwich pieces end to end on the table to make a train. Set veggies and fruit on top for cargo.
- Make Airplane Salad: Cover a plate with leafy lettuce. Set a peach half on top to make the body of the plane. Set an apricot half on each side to make wings. Insert raisins into the peach on both sides to make passengers in the windows. Place round crackers at the fronts of the wings to make propellers.
- Buy weighted cups used for drinking liquids in cars, fill them with a favorite drink, and give them to the kids. Let them keep the cups.

## FAVORS

- Send guests home with small cars, trains, or airplanes.
- Hand out books on transportation.
- Let guests keep their car cups or give them spill-proof drink containers.
- Let guests take home the costume accessories—engineer or pilot caps, small airplane pins, or engineer bandannas.

## VARIATION

- Create a cruise ship from a large cardboard box, take it to the backyard, and let the guests get in and pretend to sail away. If you like, provide some water toys for an afternoon of water fun and games.

## HELPFUL HINT

- Give yourself enough time to collect and prepare boxes before the party. Large boxes are available at appliance stores, or you can buy them from shipping stores.

# TRIP TO DISNEYLAND PARTY

Take a trip to the happiest place on Earth—Disneyland—right in your own home! Don't forget Mickey and his friends!

## INVITATIONS

- Mickey Mouse Masks: Use construction paper and felt-tip pens to make a Mickey Mouse face, with big ears, nose, and other details. Make the face large enough to be worn as a mask. Cut out eye and mouth holes; attach a ribbon on each side so the mask ties in the back. Write party details inside the mask. Ask guests to bring the masks to the party.
- Buy Disneyland postcards at a Disney store and write party details in the message area.

## DECORATIONS

- Buy a variety of Disney party products (available at party stores), such as plates, tablecloths, hats, posters, cutouts of Disney figures, and little figurines to set around the party room.
- Hang a map of Disneyland and posters of Mickey, Goofy, and Donald at a baby's eye level.
- If you like, divide the party room into various lands, such as Fantasyland or Adventureland, or focus the room on one land, such as Bear Country or Main Street.
- Add crepe-paper streamers, balloons, and Disney toys to make the place seem like the real thing.

- Don't forget to play Disney music in the background!

## COSTUMES
- Have guests wear Mickey Mouse Masks. (See Invitations.)
- Provide mouse ears and draw whiskers with face paints.

## GAMES
- Goofy's Golf: Set up Goofy's Golf course for a round of goofy golf. Glue pictures of Goofy on paper plates. Cut away a three-inch section from the rim of the plate to provide an opening for the ball to roll onto the plate. Set the plates around the room. Give guests medium-sized balls, such as Nerf, Whiffle, or tennis balls, and have them try to hit the balls onto the plates, through the cutout openings, using fat plastic baseball bats, small brooms, or other large paddles.
- Pluto's Dog-Gone Bone: Pluto has lost his dog bone. Have the kids help him find it! Make cookies shaped like dog biscuits from refrigerator dough. Bake and cool. Hide the cookies around the party room. Let guests take turns finding a bone—one bone per guest. Guests get to eat their finds. (Poor Pluto!)
- Mickey's Maze: In a separate room, toss blankets and sheets over tables, chairs, boxes, and so on. Have guests enter the maze at one end and find their way out at the other end.

- Donald's Dodge Ball: Gather half the guests in a small circle in the middle of the room, with their backs toward the center, facing outward. Place the rest of the guests in a larger circle facing the smaller circle. Have players in the outside circle toss soft balls at players on the inside circle. If a player tags someone with a ball, the two players trade places.

## MICKEY MOUSE CAKE

1. Bake a round cake and two cupcakes following a favorite recipe. Cool and remove from pans.
2. Set cupcakes near the top of the round cake to form Mickey's ears.
3. Frost the cake and cupcakes with chocolate and white frosting to resemble Mickey's face.
4. Use a cherry for a nose, licorice for whiskers, and other candies for other details.
5. Set small Disney figures around the bottom of the cake.

## ACTIVITIES

- Disney Cookies: Roll out refrigerator dough and cut out cookies using cookie cutters with Disney shapes. Bake and cool. Let the children decorate the cookies with frosting tubes and gels.
- Where's Mickey? Cut out pictures of Disney characters and glue them onto construction paper. Insert each picture into a separate manila envelope. Gather guests and sit opposite them. Select one envelope and begin to pull the picture out, one inch at a time. Each time you reveal a bit of the picture,

let guests try to guess the character. Save Mickey for last, and keep asking, "Where's Mickey?" each time you finish with one of the pictures.

- Sing-Along: Play some favorite Disney tapes on a cassette player. Have guests sing along to all the songs. For more fun, hold up matching dolls, figures, or cutouts of the characters as they are mentioned in the songs.

## FOOD

- Make Donald Duck's Quacker Sandwiches: Spread small, round crackers with peanut butter or soft cheese. Top each with another cracker and press together.
- To make Pluto Biscuits, cut out dog-bone shapes from refrigerated biscuit dough. Bake according to package directions until lightly browned. Serve with jam.
- To make a fun-to-drink Goofy Gulp, mix together equal parts fruit juice with carbonated water. Serve with crazy straws in fancy plastic glasses. For added fun, freeze cherries in an ice cube

tray, then float the frozen ice cubes in glasses.
- Serve Mickey Mouse Strips: Shred four cups of firm cheese, such as cheddar. Sprinkle the cheese over a nonstick pan so that the cheese covers most of the surface but is not too thick. Heat the pan in a 300°F oven until the cheese melts into a thin sheet. Remove from pan with a fork and tear into strips to form cheesy mouse strips.
- Don't forget Pluto's Dog-Gone Bones (see Games) and Disney Cookies (see Activities).

## FAVORS

- Give guests mouse ears to wear home.
- Hand out small plastic Disney characters.
- Send guests home with favorite Disney books.

## VARIATION

- Rent a Disney cartoon video.

## HELPFUL HINT

- Party and toy stores are filled with all kinds of Disney items.

# WINTER WONDERLAND PARTY

Baby, it's cold outside—the perfect temperature for a Winter Wonderland Party. Just bundle up and head outside for some frosty fun.

## INVITATIONS

- Snowflakes: Fold a square sheet of white construction paper in half, then in half again and then again. Round off the edges and make tiny cuts along the folds. Unfold the fancy snowflake. Write party details around the outside of the snowflake. If you like, use a large round paper doily instead.

## DECORATIONS

- Set up a Winter Wonderland inside to greet guests before you head outside to the snow:
  - Make ice sculptures or snow-men out of large Styrofoam pieces. Or cut out snowmen from large sheets of white construction paper and tape them to the walls at a baby's eye level.
  - Hang paper snowflakes or paper doilies from the ceiling to make falling snow.
  - Set out snow play equipment, such as sleds, boots, or skis.
  - Place little snow scenes under glass on the table at each guest's spot.
  - Make place mats from snowflakes or doilies.
  - Stuff a snowsuit to make a "scarecrow" and seat it at the front door.

–Play "Frosty the Snowman" and other winter tunes in the background.

## COSTUMES

- Ask guests to come dressed in their snowsuits.

## GAMES

- Snow Race: Bundle up the children and line them up in the snow. Have them race a short distance across the yard in their snowsuits, trying not to fall down. Or pull them along on sleds and race with one another.
- Stick a Carrot on the Snowman (instead of Pin the Tail on the Donkey): Build a short snowman, about the size of the guests, and decorate him with a hat, muffler, and face—except the nose. Have guests take turns (with eyes closed) trying to place a carrot nose on the snowman's face.

- Snowball Toss: Line up the children and give them each some snowballs. Set empty milk cartons on a picnic bench or a cardboard box and have the kids try to knock the cartons over with their snowballs.

## ACTIVITIES

- Build a Silly Snowperson: Build the foundation for a snowperson at the children's level. Then provide some silly accessories, such as funny veggies for the snowperson's face, funny hats for its head, jewelry, shoes, wigs, purses, scarves, boots, and so on, and let the babies go

at it. Have them make as many Silly Snowpeople as they like.
- Sleigh Ride: Look in the Yellow Pages for sleigh ride services and hire a sleigh for the party.
- Colored Snowballs: Make a batch of snowballs and place them in individual bowls for each guest. Set out containers of food coloring. Give children eyedroppers; have them fill their droppers with food coloring and squeeze the color onto their snowballs. Watch as the snowball absorbs the color. If you

## SNOWBALL CAKE AND ICE CREAM

1. Make a round cake following a favorite recipe. Cool.
2. Cover the cake with fluffy white frosting.
3. At serving time, scoop vanilla ice cream into balls, roll in coconut, and place on top of the cake in a pyramid stack. Serve immediately.

like, have them make multicolored snowballs using a variety of colors.
- Make Snow Angels: Teach the kids to lie on their backs in the snow and move their arms up and down while they open and close their legs. When they get up, snow angels remain!

## FOOD

- Make guests' favorite soup in cute plastic bowls. Let them keep the bowls when they finish their soup.
- Make snow cones by whirling ice in a blender along with a cup of juice. Scoop into bowls or ice-cream cones and serve.
- Cut out cookies in the shape of snowpeople using refrigerator cookie dough. Bake and cool. Let guests decorate the cookies with frosting, candies, and sprinkles.
- Warm guests' tummies with apple cider or hot chocolate heated on the stove. Pour into mugs, cool slightly, and serve.

## FAVORS

- Give guests colorful mittens to wear home.
- Offer small snow toys, such as plastic shovels, plastic sleds, snowman props, snowball launchers, snowshoes, snow scenes under glass, and so on.
- Hand out Popsicle molds so guests can make their own when they get home.
- Give picture books about snow.

## VARIATION

- If snowy winters are not common in your area, keep the party indoors and just make believe it's snowing outside. Cover windows with paper snowflakes, decorate Styrofoam snowpeople, cover the floor with a white blanket, make icicles out of paper, and serve Popsicles for a treat.

## HELPFUL HINT

- Make sure everyone is bundled up when you go outside, but remove the extra clothing when you're back inside.

# Index

## Order Form

| Qty. | Title | Author | Order No. | Unit Cost (U.S. $) | Total |
|------|-------|--------|-----------|---------------------|-------|
| | Baby Play & Learn | Warner, P. | 1275 | $9.00 | |
| | Happy Birthday to Me! | Lansky, B. | 2416 | $8.95 | |
| | Kids Are Cookin' | Brown, K. | 2440 | $8.00 | |
| | Kids' Holiday Fun | Warner, P. | 6000 | $12.00 | |
| | Kids' Outdoor Parties | Warner, P. | 6045 | $8.00 | |
| | Kids' Party Cookbook | Warner, P. | 2435 | $12.00 | |
| | Kids' Party Games and Activities | Warner, P. | 6095 | $12.00 | |
| | Kids' Pick-A-Party Book | Warner, P. | 6090 | $9.00 | |
| | New Adventures of Mother Goose | Lansky, B. | 2420 | $9.95 | |
| | Preschooler's Busy Book | Kuffner, T. | 6055 | $9.95 | |
| | Sweet Dreams | Lansky, B. | 2210 | $15.00 | |
| | Toddler's Busy Book | Kuffner, T. | 1250 | $9.95 | |
| | When You Were a Baby | Haley, A. | 1391 | $8.00 | |
| | | | | Subtotal | |
| | | | | Shipping and Handling (see below) | |
| | | | | MN residents add 6.5% sales tax | |
| | | | | **Total** | |

**YES!** Please send me the books indicated above. Add $2.00 shipping and handling for the first book with a retail price up to $9.99 or $3.00 for the first book with a retail price of over $9.99. Add $1.00 shipping and handling for each additional book. All orders must be prepaid. Most orders are shipped within two days by U.S. Mail (7–9 delivery days). Rush shipping is available for an extra charge. Overseas postage will be billed. **Quantity discounts available upon request.**

**Send book(s) to:**

Name _____ Address _____

City _____ State _____ Zip _____ Telephone (_____)_____

**Payment via:**

❑ Check or money order payable to Meadowbrook Press
❑ Visa (for orders over $10.00 only)    ❑ MasterCard (for orders over $10.00 only)

Account # _____ Signature _____ Exp. Date _____

**A FREE Meadowbrook Press catalog is available upon request.**
You can also phone or fax us with a credit card order.

**Mail to:** Meadowbrook Press, 5451 Smetana Drive, Minnetonka, MN 55343
Toll-Free 800-338-2232

Phone 612-930-1100    Fax 612-930-1940

For more information (and fun!) visit our website: www.meadowbrookpress.com